Fadi Yousef was born in Beirut Lebanon in 1977 and immigrated to Worcester Massachusetts in 1983. He attended Worcester State College and graduated in 1999 with a bachelor degree in literature. *Flowers for the Dying Moon* is his second published work (first *The Homeless Gentleman*). He writes in a self-coined style he calls romantic existentialism. And this he does for a sense of liberating personal identity… a sense of consolation he claims no other medium provides.

Flowers for the Dying Moon

Fadi Yousef

Flowers for the Dying Moon

Vanguard Press

VANGUARD PAPERBACK

© Copyright 2024
Fadi Yousef

The right of Fadi Yousef to be identified as author of
this work has been asserted by him in accordance with the
Copyright, Designs and Patents Act 1988.

All Rights Reserved

No reproduction, copy or transmission of this publication
may be made without written permission.
No paragraph of this publication may be reproduced,
copied or transmitted save with the written permission of the
publisher, or in accordance with the provisions
of the Copyright Act 1956 (as amended).

Any person who commits any unauthorised act in relation to
this publication may be liable to criminal
prosecution and civil claims for damages.

A CIP catalogue record for this title is
available from the British Library.

ISBN 978 1 80016 927 2

*Vanguard Press is an imprint of
Pegasus Elliot Mackenzie Publishers Ltd.*
www.pegasuspublishers.com

First Published in 2024

**Vanguard Press
Sheraton House Castle Park
Cambridge England**

Printed & Bound in Great Britain

Dedicated to the Yousef family

Contents

The Mourning	11
Crucifixion of a Flower	13
Cemeteries	15
Waiting	16
Your Name	18
The Kept	20
Life is Good	23
Light	26
Just Passing Through	28
Dawn at the Park	30
The Center	32
Ancestors	34
The Stare of a Genius	36
Hope	38
Poppy Field I	40
Poppy Field II	41
In the Womb	42
In the Night the Flowers Sleep	44
Memories of a Lover	46
To Wait	48
The Apple Orchard	50
The Trees	52
Accept	54
I Choose You	57
Concrete Wings	59
Snow Day	61
How Can I Love You	63

Time	65
Here	68
All is Forgotten	70
Fruit	72
The Garden	74
Music	76
My Mother's Angels	79
The Mind	81
I Step into the Purple	83
The Ocean	86
Woman Running	90
The Sky	92
Chair in the Sun	94
Learning to Talk	96
One Soul	99
You are all I Need	101
Dance	103
Mother	106
Poetics	108
The Prodigal Word	111
Verdict of the Bumblebee	113
Putin	116

The Mourning

Those who mourn
Must distance themselves from smiles
And take cover under black clouds and cloth
Made of midnights.
And all must hide their perfect white music…
Hide their soft melodic humming instrument
And replace the white steed of enlightenment
With the horsepower
Of black blooded mares
That guard graves.

I've come to visit with you
Because I am without you.
To come closer to the root of
My memories of you.
I've come to revisit all your
Onomatopoeias… your "Hey. Pssst"
Before you told me all your secrets…
One by one
Tiny closets in you that needed dusting
That you kept closed during the day
And opened on lovely nights

When the sun took a long wink.

Now that I've lost you
You can't be disturbed.
Your peace is engraved on stone…
Having made a name for yourself
In a cemetery without borders
That holds the lives of the dead.

The dead now know
There is no more room for them.
They have outgrown their flesh and blood…
And have given them as hand-me-downs
To a new infant with old breath.

Crucifixion of a Flower

Velvet leaves spread open like a T,
Praying for their sins.
Petals like a thorny crown
Dripping with blood.
Roots intertwined pointing
To a missing Mother Earth. The body…
The stem cell baring its green
Heaving chest. The face of the flower
Blushing with pain… looks with
Thirst towards the heavens
That has swallowed the rain.

The dead accept them. The dead
Trade their lives for flowers.
Cemeteries are oceans with
Alien islands holding forgotten
Conversations and promises.
Funerals are marriages
Between red and black roses.
And gravestones number
Your first and last words.

The amount of flowers you get
Are measured in weight… like gold.
No one knows that they are your
Bargaining chip for your date
With heaven.

Cemeteries

Homes in the dark.
Like a neighborhood left without electricity
After a storm. Houses which house
Stillness… with roots that reach black promises.
Islands of personal perfection
That have reached speechlessness… nothing
Left to say. Cities of missing communication
Where eyes go to visit flowers in vases made of
Earth.

You can hear the quiet hum of the past.
The orchestra of the dead play on. They pluck
On strings like you would a fruit
In an orchard of bones.

Those who visit have yet to accept
That only memories still live. They try to
Resuscitate the dead with their tears.
Silence is the parent of the dead. They need
No other. They are content… sleeping on their
Bed of immortal roses and concrete pillows.

Waiting

Light longing for home
To slowly stretch its arms
On its deathbed
And fill a grave.

A flower waiting to explode
into the heavens; to give birth
After generations of rooted petals…
Waiting for the extinction of its scent
In a cave.

To slowly watch the clocks
Running a timeless marathon.
With no room for unripened fruit
That falls too soon… prematurely failing.

Those without hope
Have no voice for the hummingbird.
Its wings are still… stiller than timeless
Flutter.

Where are you in the end… the end you

Search for. I will stop here you say. Or here…
And send men out to fight war against dust…
Only to be outnumbered by timeless
Timepieces that measure
The secreted secrets.

A child falls and scrapes his knee and cries out.
Mother rushes to deliver kind words and a
Band-Aid. Father keeps silent reading the paper.
At night the boy will hide behind the red barn
And pick at the scab and make sure he hasn't left
Any pain behind. Blood is beautiful in the dark…
As it slowly trickles over the knee and under the stars…
Stars that have all the time in the world…
As the boy looks up to the heavens to say,
"Look Father. I, too, bleed."

Your Name

Your name you chisel every day
In the marble air. The title
God gave you so others know
It's you who is born and cries
On a Tuesday at 9.28 a.m.
And you that has expired
Into the quiet indifference
On a Saturday evening
With its crisp September air.

Your name belongs to your dream.
They pin your name tag on it
When it is achieved and you breathe.
Names also belong to lovers.
They initially notch initials
Into the living bark
With its blind leaves.
"You are mine. We must make
A ceremony of marriage. And have a funeral
For your last name."

When someone calls your name

You hope for all things good
And despise sad news. "Mother,
Your mother has passed. Sit
At the kitchen table and cry. It is your name's
Turn to weep… because the wheel has spun
In the turmoil of the sun. And has fallen
On a bankrupted heart that belongs
Beautifully to you… without making a fuss."

Everything known has a name. Even
The unknown, which we massacre
With our letters. And hang on our hangers
Like a noose around their necks
And place it in our closets below the shelf
Holding the arrogant dictator dictionary.

The Kept

Coins and stamps can be kept.
The longer they keep dust and age
The better… the beautiful
And worthy moss.

Trees cannot be kept. They don't belong
To anyone. Only the photosynthesis
Of filtered light. Light that gives its
Rings yearly… placing them
On her rooted fingers.

A smile slips from keeping.
It fades from joy into a garden
Of nameless emotions…
Only to reincarnate
On another face

A picture must keep its frame…
An unexpiring universe within
A universe… an island
In the waters of your eyes.

The endangered flower keeps hoping
That hands will keep to themselves
And let the sun keep its schedule
For another infinity.

Blood is hard to keep. It always wants
To run away from home… like
The prodigal son who never returns…
And keeps in the night.

Words are difficult to keep. We get
Mixed up in the detailed grammar
Of meeting your lover
On the park bench
To discuss keeping
A promise of engagement.

Time. Time keeps us all. We are all
Its children. It hugs us with its hands
That keep sunrise and sunset. To rush
Or relax… to or with a glass of wine…
That has kept time since its birth…

You can not keep silence in your mouth.
The tongue keeps tripping… neglecting
To keep its word caged behind barred teeth
That gnash.

Memories. Memories keep well

The more you practice them. You can
Resurrect the dead from wherever they be.
Make them rise like baking bread
That you tear open with your hands
And examine the many caves
That hold monks praying
Over an open fire; the smoke rising
Like steam in the face of dawn.

Life is Good

Life is good.
Drink in the marrow
Of the sapling.
With your eyes
Measure the light.
Alone, break bread and make
A toast… between you
And the priests
Of many merry gods.
Bury your heart
With each passing day…
Knowing you will receive one anew
In the next morrow. Stretch your bones
Into the light
And likewise in dark…
Knowing that both
Will converse and return in mid night
Holding unknown, new fruit
From the horizon
Of uninhabitable sorrow
Set free like a caged bird
After years of held wings.

There are different degrees of light
Different shades of promise.
Light that shines in through the window
Carrying angels on its dust.
And dying light of dusk
That reads the story of day
Putting the roses to sleep.

Life is good
Because we each have a name
Your combination of letters,
Picked from the orchard of souls.
Letters which keep safe your attention…
Only known by those who know
The address
Of your personal sadness.

Greet and live
In the resurrection of spring.
And die faithfully
In the drone of winter…
Falling pieces of bewilderment
A puzzle to the eyes.
And make a man of snow
Staring at its eyes of
Infinite diamonds.
Chunks of black blind coal
That burn

With a fire whose flames reverberate
Flickering like vocal chords
In a fragile song of white-winged angels
The notes falling away like the years.

Light

Boneless rays of sun.
The rooster's first yawn
In the aborted night.
The tsunami of bright morning
On the green field
Where poppies intoxicate
The red air. The weather vane
Points to nowhere
Surrounded on all sides
By the early humdrum
Of Sunday. The light clangs
Off the church bell
As I surely pull the rope
Of angel hair.

I wipe my brow
Of sweat
And exhale the exhaustion.
My faith is heavy and wet
Like yesterday's rain
Because I am yet young of days
And the devil in the barn

Has yet to tamper with me.

The chair in the living room
Leans back with light on its lap…
Proud and entitled
To have such a guest
Even for just a while
Until the sun rests elsewhere
Before retiring for the day.
And the pirate moon takes off
His eyepatch and charges forth into
The night… steering towards war…
Into the dropping bombs of morning's rays
Where both will classically clash…
And the birds will scatter to sing elsewhere.
Fadi yousef 3/16/2022

Just Passing Through

A disheveled angel walking through; lost
And dining on the light of a street lamp
Plucking the edible rays in the night of
Nights… its eyes longing
For the blue dressing of day.
Its wing tips drag dirty
On the concrete graveyard
Belonging to black angels.

A slight rain pops up
And wings get wet and heavy…
Heavy with the doubt of
Ever reaching home.
The angel weeps. Its tears blossom
Heavenly daisies of hope
Between the cracks.

The angel follows the penniless
Path towards the park where it will secure
Until morning; until reinforcements
Flood the dawn bringing blood of
Blessings. But until then

It must hide its beating heart
Of white glowing Alleluias
From the stirring eyes of princely stars
And from the captain moon of motionless
White ladies of the dark
That desire to slowly dine
On the warmth of unfortunate halos.

Dawn at the Park

Street lights give way to the sun
And the blue replaces the sea of black stares.
Animals walk their animals.
And sound stretches and yawns.
The lake begins to smile with its ripples.
Trees unfold their silence; their leaves
Coming home to the sun; awakening…
Undressing from their black robes… while
Grass in early December
Decides to split past
Into the great mind of slumber
Before naked snow dresses the park in
Nudity… addressing your eyes
With kind, white secrets.

The houses surrounding the lake
Yet sleep to the clock. But I can see sparse
Sparks of stars through their windows… winking at me
From the kitchen, from the bedroom…
Winks like tiny seeds that will grow
Into the pattern of day.

A girl jogs by bypassing the ducks.
The air is dead and cool. A tree no longer living
Asks "Why?" I stare at its quest
From the middle of my mind… where it grows.
I have no answer to profound its ceasing.
I look up. Two birds fly in mid conversation.
We are not doomed.

The Center

This is the myriad he is at the center of.
This is the heart; the marriage
Of north, south, east and west; the pioneer
Of the thick middle. The thousands of midnights
In the night that push the borders of time
Like a body stretching; bullying the marble
Experience of the whore in the common... selling
Umbrellas in the night... in the milky galaxy
That rests in peace.

Two cats pass each other.
In between they are queens that speak
Of special loyalty to purple crowns.

There is a stress in the universe. The stars explode
Motionless under the quiet blanket...
Sleeping without a perfect pillow. A company
Of comets scream across the river, gargling in
Black holes that feed on white lightning.
The years swallow each other like circularity
Of a snake feeding on itself... like December
Taking in January

As sickness preys on healthy white blood cells
That imprison holidays that lose age with every
Coming year… finally dying in the embrace
of two lovers surrounded by the sculpture of air
Leaving one last breath in the lungs
That collapse in the end… leaving a single star.

Ancestors

The red and white church beats on time
With a rhythmic heat. I have loved a hundred…
A thousand lovers. And lost them all with a single look…
A single smile… a lost wink.
It is not in the mind, but rather the
Tongue that splits the night. The rolling hills
Of the m… the roof of the r holding the rooster hostage
To keep the dawn from coming… from breaking
The cockamamie mornings.

The rake in the barn longs to slowly stretch the winter
And sleep until the antique August yellows the tulips
That ruffle the roots of the air, the sun, the angel
Wing. The first fire belongs to priests… an accidental
Prayer to marry flesh and sun in the east… a river of
Warmth to touch the bones of winter's snow…
Where love notes were etched with dry stems. And the
Saved bloom of the rose patched the valleys.

Male caves house females. Without a door
To the open heart. Music was a chore to keep the night.

The stars applauded in the rising stands. The distant
Moon, kept lit, guards against the bored bodies
Of black matter of the future… keeps us from naming
The days that clocked time that never seems to run
   out…
Like the breath of the last hunt.

The Stare of a Genius

I see
The violence of a violet violin playing a concerto of
    algorithms
Concerning the last push without second-hand thought.
A security of sessions between rest and the family of
madness made brilliant.
A dissident dissection of sanity to please the gods of the
Frozen grandeur. To read ceramic tiles like a book of
    pictures
And repaint paintings in the dark dawn of caves BC.

Or

Panting petals in a field of fire slowly deceasing and
Three-legged horses in a race… but learning
To lean on one another. The story of a stone bridge
Telling stories of east crossing west… bridging sun
And moon; making friends out of tiny enemies.
Teeth like ruins war against the dentist of time
That chews on flesh. And fleshy flowers throw
Alleluias at the foot of the church.

At this point in time the clock lags. The bloom of time
    slows
Down. A single neuron burning. The final candle.
A kiss between lovers with nothing in between

That endures its stay and delivers the last frozen see
When you tear open the fabric window and ask, "When?
　　Where? Why?
How? We live on this oxygenic substance." With
Lungs like angel wings that beat in flight…
With no room for mistakes.

Hope

A perfect reed quivering…
Fine tuning the air
The circumference.
A light pointing forward
Into the dismal dark
Of unknown ghosts
Of measure.
To slowly sip
On the morning
And stretch your vision
Beyond the night
Of many blind pines.
To love love
And love the word love.
The singular distance
The bipolar substance
Of the heart.
And to not know
What to do
With old roses…
Maybe they will hang on,
By their leaves,

Another day
In the sky blue
Vase, as light runs away
From their thorns
As to not bleed
Into the field
Of the common man.
To grow from knowing
Into not knowing
Like a gentle breeze
That swirls in place
Ruffling the hair
Of the tree…
Gentle in autumn yellow.
The leaves charging
Like already dead soldiers
Into winter.

The horizon of peace
Is always out of reach.

Poppy Field I

I dragged you
On my back
Like a cross
Through the intoxicating
Poppy fields
Through the red blooded
Petals of peaceful hunger
And the yellow center satellites
Frozen in prayer
In the cosmos of the field
Where the heart falls apart.

Poppy Field II

Holding the hand
Of her faithful mother
The girl walks
Through the poppies
Safely underneath
The sun umbrella
In her dress of white
Wondering wonderful
Weight… dragging
The afternoon behind her
As it clings to the horizon
Walking into the moon
As it is… wherever it is
As large… at large
Swallowing swallows
From midfield
Where she walks
Gingerly
As to not disturb
The sleeping
Drugged flowers.

In the Womb

In the womb of the valley
Where the tulips grow
He walks thinking gargantuan thoughts…
Pushing back the mountains
That yield to his balance.

He takes his time
Stealing their time
As to understand
The misunderstood
Creatures of nature…
The hare that splits
The air between its ears
Unsure about the unstable hunger
Of the snake
And the eagle
Which digest the heart of finality
Hiding in a snowfall
With its white lies
And the frozen front
Of the wood's edge.

The tip of his vision
Visits the mountain tops
That hold up the circle sky
As it publishes purple storms
Weather of seldom words
For rare eyes of rarities that wed.

The echoes are not heard
In the past silence…
Only the presence of a future grand
To be anesthetized in a painting
With no time for butterflies.

In the Night the Flowers Sleep

In the night the flowers sleep slowly
Secreting black beauty
While the day dreams.
I've seen nothing
To change my mind
About noon
And the innocent children
That hide there upon high
Where the single song
Is bellowed and bought
By abstract men
Sitting atop sagging horses…
Cutting through the windows
Of the valley.

Light is the enemy
Of sacred black blooms
As clouds ship midnights
From horizon to horizon
The fragile cargo
That weathers the storm…
Separating and merging

Like time leaving time
And joining once again.

I have faith…
Sent from the east.
It has traveled far
To touch the western chamber
Of my mystical heart
That drinks and wines willingly
Until my soul is drunk
Underneath the flower
Of which I pluck the petals, repeating,
"She loves me. She loves me not",
Until I run out of time to love
Leaving only the center for hope.

Memories of a Lover

The memories are all around you.
Like the crooked sign
On the street that reminds you
Of the crook that stole your heart.

And the papers on your desk
That take you back
To his love notes
Are in smooth cursive…
Without gaps
Just the way you miss him.

Remember the fruit
On your table…
The peaches that went bad
Like your heart after he left…
The pit still in your throat.
And the indigestible heart
Breaking in every room of your house
That remind you
As you try to leave them and forget
The flowers … the cards he gave you

They were such a cheater's wink.

You're alone now
To mire and revisit
The burning romantic neurons
Of grey matter; shades of grey
Like his indecisive half kisses
That rented your heart for just a while
But never bought the home
Where your love abides.
What a crush it is
To feel the weight of the wait
And to know you are not loved
But just flailing
In the winds of others' indecisions
Winds that no longer have strength
To mate and hold creatures of flight.

But your plight
Continues still
And in bed in mid sleep
Your arm still reaches for his ghost.

To Wait

The birds will have to wait
To feed on time
When the clock stops
For the golden branch.

There are no birds
Circling on one wing
While the full gull hovers
And glides down the neck of the swan.

The trees are behaving in the speechless cold
As winter passes through their hair
Holding spring by the root
To be planted in the grand
Resurrection of the quiet.

The waves in the water
Are of one family
Holding hands
To celebrate their full reunion
On shore where I walk freely
On the sand that has no religion…

And knows only about hosting man
On its shoulders
The tongue-tied ocean lapses over and over...
Waiting for a reply.

The Apple Orchard

In the space of the apple orchard
The trees are galaxies
Of which you pluck a planet
And bite with gravity
Down on the equator
Where the ripe heat lives
In the juice of the orb.
The boneless flesh
Sweet with white light
Makes its way down
To the root of your hungry satellites
As fall falls in the dark
Felling the universe
Down to the fabric of earth
Open to all
Without borders or gates
Welcoming humans
To shoot across
Like comets or freeze
Like stars
Or swallow like black holes
The living worm in the core

Which will take years
to digest.

We harvest the seed
And plant it in the bowl to rest
On the versed table.

The Trees

The trees are sad and in rags.
They are homeless and without season or reason
To hold anything… not even birds
Plain of color or song. The trees have been wronged
And held from breeze or wind or whatever belongs
To take flight from there. The bark is mute
Like a dog hung in plain sight of day. A few leaves
Hang for later… unable to be reached
By half a winter's wind.

The willow tree accepts the season
And is as nude as an angel
Caught bathing in the fountain,
changing into its morning wings.
While actors walk by rehearsing
For spring.

The snow comes slow
Like a song at first
And then into a full-blown opera
With all its madness and pompous players.
The patient audience is caught deep

In wonder; in stages of amazement
To the enveloping environment.
Some search for the exit to the open heart
Of the resting park
Some rush the stage to join
The blizzard with its white teeth.
Others charge their memories of childhood
And dance with the flakes
That fall in love
As they kiss the ground.

Accept

Accept life the way it is.
Accept the honest plight
Of the honey lily
Searching for the truth
Of perfect peace
To find rest
In a gentle pillow
Breezing by in a dream.

Accept the waiting
Of her humble heart
Waiting for a kiss
From his lips
As he returns from war
Holding foreign blossoms
Which she feels the thorns of
On the sides of her comely breasts
That pulse for his hands
Like parentheses around the battle
Of friction between them.
A battle he always comes away the victor
After conquering her land daily

A never-ending frontier
To capture her heart
And take hostage her eyes.

Accept the single rose
In the lowly valley
Between the woods
And the waters
That hold hands
In the midst
Catching the tears
Of the mountains
Crying in the distance.

Accept the madness
Of the missing
Caught deep
In Mississippi waters
Imported from clouds above
That rest in the mist.

And accept that which is true
Between your eyes
And mine. Like the first kiss
A first star
In black memory…
Before you made yourself known
To me.
Between sunrise and sunset

Before I came to know
The map of your heart
With all its deep dangerous waters
Where I go
Fishing for your truths
That never surface
To your kissing lips.

I Choose You

I choose you
To hold hands with…
To share the infinite details
Of the coursing light of day.
Oh to walk miles
On the map
Of your face
To reach the X marks the spot
And treasure the moment
Where your smile
Crosses mine.
I choose you
To sing with,
You and I,
To empty our lungs
Into the sensual night
Into the exhaling
Mother Earth we have exhausted.

Here comes your heart
To visit my lonely heart
Carried on a breath

Drowning
In the endless
Lost hours of trembling.
Here you are
On my lips
Searching for your lips…
A primitive promise
To one another.
Your kind eyes
Find birth
In my eyes
And I know
I love you
Because I forever find
Your royal roses
Blooming in the garden
Where I pray.

Concrete Wings

I cannot fly
With these concrete wings.
I cannot love you
With this heart of stone.
I cannot feel
In this steel winter.
I am a bard of hope's ignorance…
Carrying knowledge
Of the paper knife
That cannot cut
Through your smooth night
Of unsettling memorials to dead
Statues of lovers.

Blue hills surround my imagination
And I travel the endless purple cloudscape
That rape my purse of good standing.

Everyday I learn and unlearn…
Lock and unlock
Your next beautiful step
Careful not to tread

On the treadmill of hope
That leads to nowhere… where
All of a sudden I find
My daily God
That leads me to sleep
And promise rest from thinking
Until I wake
In the coffin of morning
And unravel myself
From the maze of night
Where flowers wilt and die
In the shadow
Of your eyes
Of exponential bliss.

But I live still
To swallow the evidence
Of your love that drips like the sun…
Counting fuel-less time
That forever burns.

Snow Day

It's a snow day
And the snow banks
Are bankrupted in white.
I am no longer here nor there
But caught in the middle
Of the snowflakes.
And the snowman's imagination is blank.
School is closed
But the children study
Joy and smiles
Sliding down the dead chaos
Forgetting their limbs
On the ground in angels
That fly past the limited roofs.
The apocalyptic adult shovel is deafening
As it scrapes the mindful driveway.
Fresh fallen heavy light
Has become tangible
And digits are counted
And numbered
On mittened fingers.
The happy heart

Cannot be measured
In feet or inches.

After the fall
The silence is chased
By the sun.
I am neither here nor there
But always caught falling
Between those two faces.

How Can I Love You

The whole world is talking about love.
Yes. That is what they are talking about.
That is what they are saying.
That is the whole conversation.
How to get it? How to keep it?
We are all biblical actors of courtship.
Kings and queens of our endless hearts.
Slaves to the hunger
Of emotional imagination.
Where is your touch my love?
On what snagging twig
Did you lose your smile
That was meant for me.
Where is that earthly thief
Of the sensual senses
That missed my fingered destination.
Bring home… the vessel of your blood
Closer to mine
So we can pour full
Fluid nights together
Overflowing in our glasses.
Without cumbersome clothes

Of the disturbing day.

You bring dawn
And I will bring dusk.
You bring the sun
And I will bring the moon.
Sunrise and sunset too bring.
And we will hang them on the bedpost
Until the end of these eyes.
Until we no longer seek days.
Until the beasts in us
Are tamed and subside.
And we rise
And put them on again
To join civilization
Only to search for one another once more
Bringing what we've learned
About this romantic language
This never-ending configuration
Of arms and legs around each other
In this our never-ending romance novel
That we take turns reading to one another
Without looking at the hindering time
That tries to catch us naked of our names.

Time

You can't trust time.
It has many faces.
From the bossy clock in the kitchen
Or the watch on your right hand
That's always right.
From your sleeping bedroom
To the tyrant time keeper
In the dozing living room.
The center of the sun is heated
And shadows the grandfather clock
Where dust has died
But still snores noisily
In formal pressed suits
To awaken again wide eyed
With the wet dripping rag
To be carried out the winded window
Where butterflies drunkenly flutter
Sliding like butter on the hot sweating breeze.
To the left. To the right…
Timely hands awaken and employ
The rusty swing in the rusty yard
Bumping into the laying horizon

That lays in bed
And returning once again from the edge
As the child cries joy
For the long adventure
Between the strict three and nine.
The second hand chases
And swallows its parents
That stumble slow.
Too old to hurry for anybody's schedule.
But still young enough to exercise
Here and there
Mindless appointments in molded clay
A perfect recipe set forth since blind birth
That winds drearily down
Till death treats you
To strip yourself down
Of numerical mountainous words
And you find the tilled treasure
That you have not expired too early
Or too late
But just in time
For your final funeral
When mourners mangle and show up
Running a little behind. They
Know you can't complain with caresses.
Their tears fill the abyss of their sad brim
For just a moving moment
Before time tells them that it is enough
And they need to shuffle along.

The crowd daintily disperses.
Some are early. Some are late.
But their legs keep keeping time.
Left. Right. Left. Right.
Tic tock. Tic tock.
Somewhere in between
We live and die.
Somewhere in between
We continue to breathe.
Yes. Somewhere in between
Where the sun slowly surely
Freely changes color. Too far
From imprisonment of tiny timepieces
That click like an empty gun
Blowing you away
Like dust on heaven's vase
That waits for a flower
Named after you.
Where you hope you can finally find
A rupturing rest
From the need to love and be loved.
So. What is the name of your flower?
Bewilderment perhaps. Or
Melancholy Maze. How about
Sad Rainbow. I know mine.
But it's only communicable
In the silly silences
When your heart is happy
And
Leans against the shoulder of my soul.

Here

Here I am safe
In the gentle memory of summer.
The swing sways empty
And the children do not play.
Absence is king
In the age of the weeds
And unruffled breath.
The sun bears the seldom key
Of locked time.
And the bones of the melancholy skeleton
Are still… simply weathered
In honest nature.
The blunt seasons have become uniform
Thirsty and parched
For the surmise of indifference.
The scarecrow too is dull
And full of lies
To the lingering lily
That searches for surprise
In the bored cavity of the face
That inhales endless; a habit
Hard to break

Like a bird's beak
Pecking at the humility
Of blue's hum.

The property of the scene
Is numbered
And lives in ends
Sentenced to hang
From the horizon
Where death's normality
Will announce the news
To the unending side of sighs.

The globe will weep
For the loss of the last member
Leaving without echo
Or mention
Which the dry well
Will surely miss…
Disturbed about the loss
Of its often-comer
A well-wisher that has succumbed
To the leaning purpose of earth.

All is Forgotten

There is nothing to see here.
Nothing to hide.
Not even a question.
There are no answers
For the red red wagon
Wagging its tail.
No red red rust
On the green green grass.
The vision is absent. Absolutely.
No questionnaire for the quiet.
The red barn is not in shambles.
Is there a barn? Do you see it?
Have you seen it? With its chipped paint?
The roof of the barn is not on fire
Under the sun.
The chickens do not lay eggs
That roll down the steep roof of the barn.
The rake too is unemployed…
Laid off against the side
Of the missing barn.
And the shovel
Didn't have its lip below the earth

Between the present and the dead.
Resting its arm against the tree
That was just about to leave
In the season
That never came
To call your forgotten name.

Fruit

The fruit cannot be eaten.
They are missing in rest
In the Ming blue bowl
Having an off day. Cannot be held
With hands made of soil and earth.
Hands that bring water to the face
After toiling in the field
Harvesting God's delightful candy.

The matrix of the peach
Cannot be eaten
While leaning against the tree or sun
Wiping peach juice from your mouth like sweat
Saying, "Geez. This is hard work."

The grapes have been abducted.
Stolen away into far away satellites
Of green and red homes of wine.

And the wide-hipped pears of women
Are practicing giving birth to twins. They labor
In the field to reach your table.

It begins to rain in the living room
And the bowl on the table fills with water
It begins to sink into the ocean of memories
Like a boat
Carrying precious cargo to your mouth.

The Garden

The shovel's lower lip
Is curving the underworld.
The handle is holding up the tree
Of Newton's apple.

The gardener is resting his sweat.
His gloves are off
After his fight with the chrysanthemums.
A knockout punch
Below the belt of the horizon.

The soft soil is accepting applications
For footsteps
That the rain will recall
Years from now
In an archaeological dig
That will unearth
The sniffing hound.

The flowers are hosted
By the arborvitae's roundabout.
A crowning of jewels

As in the petals of the sunflower
Presenting the face
Of man's seed of the billionth sun.

There is a woman in the lawn chair.
She is leaning back
Her legs are crossed
Like two thick intertwined roots
Leading up to a hidden pool in between
Where Medusa bathes
With her head of snakes shifting
Turning a man's virile member into stone
That splits releasing her slithering children.

Music

A string in the air
Floating on a dreaming bed
Sailing from shore to shore
Leaving the sound bay of your mouth
To wake up at the island of your ear.

Deft filaments of voice reaching
From cup to cup. Humming
In the distance. A hummingbird
On a wire between two houses
Or a band of houses
In a neighborhood of instrumental organs
Of the plucking and winded body.

Two hands. Each hand with an ensemble
Of five fingers finely strumming
The late summer chords of evening
Thirsting for sultry song. Your arm
Around her latest evolution of herself…
Her love… playing you like a fiddle
That you gladly dance to.

Don't Touch Anything

Don't touch anything.
Don't let your nose touch
The rose you inhale
For the scent of the blessings

Don't let your eyes touch
The depth of the woods
With its black velvet curtain.
Lest your eyes become tainted
And lost in the abyss.

Don't let your ears touch
The church bells ringing
In the river
Calling the salty fishermen
From preaching to the fish
On the banks
And their wives rushing
Over the hills
Still wearing their apron
Around their waist
Over their Madonna blue garment
Singing to the flowers
That sway themselves
Like waving arms of the choir.
The children run past breakfast
With innocence behind their ears

That never came out in Holy Water.

Don't touch the cross
With dirty fingers
Lest they reach the altar
And stain heaven
With unwashable sin.

Don't chew on the communion bread
With a mouth that has eaten stale rabid bread
And drunk wine of leisure
Causing yourself to pass
On the Truth of the both.

Don't let your knees touch the ground
As you pray
But let your hands split the heavens
To receive from God's cabinet
That which is untouchable.

My Mother's Angels

My mother's curtains in the living room
Are dressed around the window
Like white angels.
They filter the light that comes in.
They guide our sight as we look out to the sky
To heaven.
They keep in the warmth
And keep out the cold.
They see that our day is blessed
In morning
And guard against the black of night.
Mom always makes sure the angels' wings
Are clean and pressed.
The ruffle of them always looks
Like they will fly away any minute
Especially when the wind blows
Through the open windows.
But they never leave her…
Mother keeps a lovely home for them.
Mom always loves her angels.
They are like her children
She keeps fed with joy and praise.

Everyone who comes always comments on them
They say,
"Oh Mona, what beautiful children you have."

The Mind

A man's best friend
A man's worst enemy.
Limitless space.
The desert of the nomad.
And the prisoner's cell.
A scream without walls...
Without an echo of understanding...
God's canvas for peace and madness.
Grey matter between black and white.

A stream... cutting through the woods...
A stream of consciousness... littered with
Rocky dreams on the banks
That you hopscotch from
Thought to thought.

I don't mind
If you imagine me
Under the sunny star
Traveling to the depths
Examining the tip
Of each and every neuron

Like a frontiersman visiting
The roots of your genius
And the reaches of your hoping…
But also your cancerous routines
That harden and cement
The chains of your mad habits.

Look for something new
Without reaching for yourself.
Something that has escaped your mind
And landed in your heart
Where tales are told of the spirit…
That intangible being that nor
Eats nor sleeps but feeds
On the currency of the soul
Which leaves you rich or poor
From moment to moment
But always leaves you…
Leaves you wandering in wonder
About catching your next
Train of thought
Before it leaves the station
Without you
Headed east towards the temple
Of original thought
Where the mind feeds.

I Step into the Purple

I step into the purple wood.
Gentle and unassuming.
Without making a difference.
Without leaning into
Or away from
A palpable sadness or
Steadfast beauty.
Without whispering a wind
Into the ear
Where peaceful creatures sleep
In their beds
At ready to come to life
Into the puzzle of day.

This same wind
Parents a breeze
That wanders the halls
Of this same wood
Delivering the message
That breath still breathes.

And let it be known

That the face of this wind
Has traveled the earth
To reach the thankless valley
That is without emotion
And stares into a deft rustle
Of motion.

And let it still be grieved
This passing of the days
And this brave gravity
Let it play its role
With the roses that resist the rain.
And let it take its toll
On the trees that willfully reach
Past their allowance.
And this growth of deep velvet, let it
Sit and perplex man's dexterity
So full of awe.

Mother and daughter have reached
The valley of sighs
Where they pluck tulips unhurried
Coaxing them to their nostrils
Before putting them to sleep
In the basket.
They step tenderly
As to not misstep
And disrupt the quiet day
Where lies prey on the living.

The sun strikes
Tween noon and night.
A change in color blushes the sky.
A split from above
Brings the lightning.
Thunder rolls like a chariot
Through the valley.

The mountains are pregnant
With smoke. Victory cometh soon.

But first
A whisper of leaves… just a whisper
So as to mourn
This corrupt sky.

The Ocean

A reflection of many faces.
The reflex of thirsty eyes.
Thousands of smiles
Chasing a calm release on shore.
A marathon of sprinting tides
Following the tugboat moon.

The home of many living creatures,
Deep and shallow,
Of hidden time and lurking loss…
And of vibrant color of silver steel
And pools of rainbow creations.

You can rest on the island… finally.
And breathe in the search
Of your seldom self. Your heart can
Beat here. And your ears will listen to the
Quiet. Sit on the shore… on the edge of
Civilization. And stare at what you need to
Know and say. Stare at your memory
Of the mechanical metal machine
Of schedules and appointments

Dressed and pressed
For constant disappointment…
Where your laughter travels to die
Over and over like so many waves.
A consistent let down
Of revelation. Where your heart
Roasts over the open fire
Of false fullness.

Sit on the beach made
For one… no room for talk
Or false motion…
Or smooth plastic smiles…
No time for over energetic young girls

That easily give life.

But you.
I will wait for you.
I will wait until your heart beats close…
Until my heart hears yours
And my eyes seek your cheeks to separate
And tire from over-smiling.
Sit. Sit a while. Talk. Talk a while.
Tell me of your heartache and joy…
Of your pleasure and sorrow.
I will listen. I promise.
Until we die together…
From overexposure to *love*

A word weary from being pulled
Here and there
At whimsy of clumsy magic
Of little boys toying with the gods.

I'm ready. I'm ready for you…
We don't have to talk. Even if we do,
I will not hear the words. Just
Their weight in sadness
Or the pull in their gladness
The red in their blood
Or the saccharine in their sweet.

So
Here we are
You and I.
Perfectly alone.
Touching without touching.
Seeing without looking
Into the eyes of the sky
Angry at us
For being so selfishly complete
Without any of the resources of the universe.

Let it all come and go. All of it.
We are happy being
And not being
Somewhere
Somehow

Existing
Naked of body.
We become of one ether
Glowing, fizzling in and out of existence
In the presence of the dark…
Aboard some vessel sailing late
Into the heart of beginning and unending
Arrhythmic retreating into the origin
Of begotten sacredness… where we die in
The arms of silence
Like two halves coming together
To form the face of God.

Woman Running

There's a woman running.
To catch a bus
Or a taxi
Or the first few snowflakes of winter.
Or to catch the world turning
Beneath her feet.

She rushes past the flower shop
Dragging the roses with her…
In her hair
In her eyes that quickly glance
At their bleeding red hearts.

She travels by the bakery
Stealing breakfast with her nose.
The monks making the dough rise
With their prayers.

She hurries past the common
Cutting straight through the middle
Of the thick crowd as two by two
They write their romance novel

That has no ending.

The woman stops at the church
For a quick moment.
She crosses herself and looks up
At the cross above. She prays she can
Stop running soon.

She gets home and runs
Into the embrace of her lover…
Into the heart of her day
That beats with a smile.
Into the welcome of her home
That holds her tight with familiarity
And belonging.

Run as she may
It's never fast enough
To lose herself
In his arms.

The Sky

Blue endless blue.
Looking for help
With its sadness.
A plume of blooming clouds
In rosy white. Fronts
Marching forth
To consult and consume one another…
In peaceful war… in quiet music.
A blanket to blanket
The sleeping earth
That dreams about us
As we hide ourselves
From God's eyes
That ask personal questions
About the heart of calmness
And about the many shades
Of possible pain peppered
With flighty birds
That hold gravity under
Winged windows of floating distance.

What of the black sky…

The knight in the dark
That searches to infest
And corrupt
The sky's good standing
That has traveled in many pieces
To become of one piece above
Which celebrates
Wearing colorful masks of storms.

I have reached the beach of the horizon
Where I rest my soul
At sky's edge
Only to question the beyond
About tomorrow
And the worries
That hold no weight
Under today's tyrant canopy
Where we shall feast
Between the parentheses
Of sun and moon…
Dining outside in union
Under the lyre and
Stars that have many names…
Where lovers go to die for a day
And awaken in the morning
That much closer.

Chair in the Sun

Panting on all four legs.
Sweating in the sun.
Waiting for weight.
Waiting for lost love.
The players of this earth
Are carved in wood
On its legs
That run out of room
To go anywhere.
And carved on its backrest
Are vines of heaven
That support imagination
And meditation that decipher
The center of dreams and dreamers
That travel while sitting still
In the mindset of rest.

Lean back.
Take in the room
And the room outside the window
That hosts kings and queens
On a quest to lose you and themselves.

But you. You are content sharing the world
With your eyes; opening and closing
Doors to adventure
With just a blink… a wink
As you set off to claim
The exotic ones
Whose hearts beat afar
Calling for you to tame their fire
As you stare into the close distance
From your lording position.

Learning to Talk

The black hole of the O opening.

The negative note of the N
That nullifies news from nowhere
Negating knowledge.

The rough roof of the R
Where the rain rolls repetitious
Above the rafters.

The gloom of the M
That mother's mountains
Missing in might where
The W takes flight with wings
Of weightless white doves
Wandering in the sky
Like many pairs
Of white cotton gloves
Wait for you to decide
Between wailings and whispers.

The capital A is an angel

At alert to assert its wings
And take to air above all assumption.

The H of heavenly hung lungs,
Which hover around the heart,
Are in the heaviness of the heaving
Chest of hope, hurrying with hunger.

And the T... crucified tall,
Takes turns testing truth
Tween east and west
Where beggars borrow prayers
To tempt the temple of time.

And then the X. X marks the spot
Of beginning and ending. Where kisses
Are lost... between my lips and yours.
Or an X-ray where hearts are caught
Beating behind the soul of the sun...
Tucked in bed behind the invisible
Where lovers disappear in the distance
Holding hands like inseparable light.

The Z is final. The zenith of zero
Where eyes take vision
From atop. The zed of that which is said
In sadness. Sad as in a team of
Boneless horses
Dying in a river

Their thick marble breath no longer slave
To the dead body. The tongue loosened,
Becomes one with the wind to speak.

One Soul

Your soul is tied up
With my soul…
For we are descendants of a prayer
That calls to be free from flesh
And join the greater spirit
That wanders the earth.

Let them call us thieves
Who have stolen
One another's hearts
And hidden them
In the vase of the valley
Where timelessness beats
At the feet of the mountains…
Where we come to meet
After the end of wars
Waged over one rib
Removed in my sleeping
When I alone was tempted.

There was no turning of time then.
No memory for dawn to awaken.
We were two flower heads

Of one single stem; children
Of one embrace in the shy sun.

There was only wind, light, and stone.
Stuff falling from the holes
Of God's pockets; mischances of
Unwritten verses of the first song
That took life miscellaneously
At his beginning behest.

This was the waking of Eden.
A time of time's yawning
When animals came tame
And walked in sophisticated manner...
And fed on faith at the gate-less spread
When history was an infant
Suckling on Eve's breast.
Before sun and moon
Were pinned on the chest of space
To illuminate the faces
Of heroes and thieves.
Before stars were sharpened
Into five points. Before God
Drew a hoping horizon
Between the ocean and sky
And set off the race
Of man's inhumanity to himself.
When God named himself with letters...
No longer anonymous.

You are all I Need

You are all I need, my love.
All I need to remember.
My consistent constant of
Burning tenderness. The purpose for my
Solitude. An undying tribute to your absence…
A memorial for a lost lover
In a war lost in love.

My soldiers weep bullets
Over the grave of your memories.
Emptying their arms of sorrow.
And even my enemies cry
For the loss of love's tomorrow…
Now washing on the beach
Of my sadness
Limbless and dead
From carrying a heart so heavy.

The world is on fire
In your missing eyes… set aflame
On a cross
Mounted on the mountain of my desire

That screams your name
To the valley
As pilgrims pilgrimage
And ascend to pay honor
To your missing smile.

I must now bury my mornings
In earth's flesh to divide my pain
Flowing in my veiny rivers of blood.
Blood darker than the blackest of sacred
Midnights
When we used to come together
To converse soul to soul. Yes. And sometimes
The silences spoke too
And touched
Creating a new language
Only we knew… that traverses
Even the furthest of distances
To kiss your living lips.
Fadi yousef 3/1/22

Dance

Painting with the body
In the pastel air.
Hair screaming in space like wildflowers.
The body burning freely in wildfires
Trying to extinguish
The rhythmic oxygen drowning
The heart beats
In throngs of color…
Earthy blue and green
Under the feet
Of the pulsing pulsar
Of fluid partners. Or single…
Like divorced love of the flower
Swaying in the eyes; a vision
Of disbelief on the canvas sky
That steps from light to light.

The marriage of movement
Between the horizon and the mind
Contemplating awe and orgasmic blush of body
Where the limbs seek freedom
From their master… no longer slaves to sleep

But free to court the curved blood
Of silhouettes.

Listen with your vision
As the instrumental toe trips triple
From star to star
From beginning to end
Springing from fantasy to fantastic
As the member gives birth
To artistic articles of sensual intimacy
A womb that cocoons the infant battles
Of seduction
With a fine brush of fading faultless fancy.

The legs like roots blossom in the face
Under circles of merry men
And wobbly women prancing at dawn
Welcoming a new forever day
To the audience of loud applauding lords
And forgetful ladies of camouflaged rouge.

The music of the body
Is written and rewritten
On the blank page of the air's tender blue sculpture.

After climaxing
The body bids adieu…
Dying in exhalation
Of one last final

Sorrowful throb of the pleasing heart.
Leaving an empty shell
Of the former self on the ground...
Walking away victorious
Ready to take the spirit
By the hand.

Mother

Proud breasts lactating love.
A hug that extends past the womb
Blinding the child from the turning turmoil.
Joy and laughter are banked in her eyes
And emerge in a kiss
As her lips rush
To doctor cuts and bruises
Of the pride and body.

She cooks with the full fire
Of the heart. And cleans the house
And soul of the devil's dust.

Her flesh is rounder than the earth.
Her laughter shakes the mountains
Free from the sky.

The horizon cries
And drowns the valley with a nurturing sorrow
At the least of our pain.

You raised us bright like the sun

And set us high like the stars. Your voice
Is the song of our yearning. Your words the ripe fruit
    plucked from heaven's orchard...
Set on the table to fill your absence.

You are the reason I walk into war; to rescue
Your honor. And place it in your temple
Where I pray to die before you
And be reborn again through your tears
To build you a house in heaven with
My hands.

Poetics

She lives in poetics.
Plucking the words
From her garden like flowers
Yellow and red
That she holds up to the sun
Like a photograph.
The light shining through the petals
As she looks for any imperfections.

Up to the sun
To smile
And put them in her basket
Full of other stemmed delights
As she mumbles to herself
And to the cut flowers
Who hear her and follow her direction
Feeling safe in her lies
As she connives and plans
To have them spend the rest of their lives
In a vase.

She prances she laughs

Without a period of doubt…
Excited to be alive
On the heavenly tender
Green grass
That fits her naked feet
Like an old comfortable shoe.

In circles she dances
Around and around
Like the rings of Saturn.
Her arms held out leaning
Inward getting sucked in
By an invisible whirlpool
Or teetering back and forth
Like an airplane
Looking to land
But never does

Her smiles sail the blue above
Like many canoes
With thousands of rowers
Yearning to reach the beach
Of her cheeks
And rest like freckles
That set up camp
And burn fires at night;
The sparks floating
And cementing like stars
That whisper to the moon

Like spies conspiring about distant lands
Of some tomorrow when they plan
To free the flowers from their cell
On the living room table

But unwittingly
they get drunk on the black silence
And stumble into morning
Where they keep in sleep
Dreaming of decorating the kingly moon
With a crown of flowers and
Anointing the queen of time
With fragrance of roses.
Fadi yousef 3/16/22

The Prodigal Word

Oh Mother
What have you done to me…
I am the latest evolution of your womb.
I sit on the sun's porch
Faded floorboards
And bored fields
That reflect the aftermath of afternoon
A prequel to dusty dusk
When devils rub their eyes
And wake for a new parenthesis of time.

There is no room for love
Only wrinkled wishes
Stillborn and grey.
The undead yawn, stretch, and walk.
Both they and the streets
Bent over and heavy-tongued
In the private ruins… stressing
The absence of affectionate touches
And lack of glimpses of the pupils
Of the sighing race.

Father darkness awaits.
Father! Darkness awaits.
Fat and gluttonous feeding
On ignorant light that blinds
The universal eye at its closing…
Where 'happiness' is always wanting…
Waiting to scratch out a name for itself.
To be proud of other more honorable
Of emotions…
To be like 'exuberant' or 'spiritless'
And to sit high on the shelf
Where God reaches up
To grab the story of the prodigal word
That never came home
To rest its bones on a page.
And take root in a divine verse.
To be the last voice heard
At the end of the book
When we close the cover
On another turning of the earth.

Verdict of the Bumblebee

Dear bumblebee
Come as you are
But not earlier than the budding sun.
Not earlier than morning's buzz.

Murmur as you do
To your blue address
As your wings tire from
Holding up both sides
Of every storied sky.

Tire from teaching children
How to walk
Away from your pointy madness.

Just the mention of your name
Freezes stampeding moments.
Black and yellow is your borrowed
Religion; as the days practice fleeing
From your fleets of flighty jargon.
Leave me be. What have I done to hinder
Your hum and your inhumane greetings…

Rushed and twisted hellos.

Bee gone. Get away. I crave you to be a
Memoir of my memory… without a rear-view
Mirror mending the past.

No I will not succumb to your bullying
Bravado. Oh be still for a moment
That I may show you my stinging boot.

Maybe then you will leave me
To be wet in the sad rain
That once weighted your wiry wisdom.

Maybe your compatriots will attempt to attack
Me in my dreams hanging on
My left brained horizon.

Well you fumbling bumble
Carry on. But carry no more your
Embarrassing tall tale
Of death's flighty finality
Now try to puncture joy.
Now try to keep my children without happy
Hearts. Try now to catch
One false witness
In the court of raw verdicts.
You will be sentenced
To a perfectly sound cell. With no room

To land on innocence.
And don't try to apologize now…
Your point has already been made.
Fadi yousef 3/19/2022

Putin

Putin
May you find unrest
With the dogged dead.
Even Satan himself has disowned you.
May your last hour of pain be patient
And come slow like the blood of soldiers
Seeping through the fabric of uniform ashes.
Bullets have blinded the sky
Raped by the insanity of your many men
Who burn their souls to keep you warm.

Believe this! Mortar will barrage your
Mother's regretful womb.
And you will have a crown of shrapnel
Placed on your severed head.

May peace of mind evade you
Like a whore walking your ruined dreams
Armed and limbless
Searching endless for extinct flowers
To dress your graffitied grave.

Refugees walk great distances
Under a murderous sun
Bridged by your spineless body.
Your demons search
High and low for refuge
From your nameless shame
Wandering the desert
Finding only salt water of dust
Of rusted wells of distrust
Reflecting the madness of your pawns.

And purposeless rain will follow you
All your days falling
Like fire on your unprovoked invasion
Where voiceless babies were left
With interrupted wishes.

With hope
All your ripe fruit will rot at your touch
And the names of crying children
Be engraved on your tombstone
And be written in braille on your hardened heart.

We will see you hang from the same line you have
Crossed. To satiate your appetite for indigestible
Land and power that are too heavy to hold
With bloodstained hands…

Your conscience will haunt your homeless

Motherland… shelterless and naked
In the eyes of the world
Whose back you have stabbed
With thirsty bayonets
Of your bastard sons…
Firing at will
Into the flesh and body of humanity
Which will rise in unison. And
Into the ear of God cry "Father. Mercy. For the smoke
 of white flags has blotted out the sun."

And He will hear us.
He will hear us
And we will beat the victory drum
With your cowardly bones
And you will dance with the serpent at your feet
to the song of the dead
As your victims will sing from heaven's balcony.

And you shall be sentenced to the abyss
to pick roses
For all the dead.